THE SOUTH WEST COAST PATH

THE SOUTH WEST COAST PATH

Adam Burton

FRANCES LINCOLN LIMITED
PUBLISHERS

Frances Lincoln Limited
4 Torriano Mews
Torriano Avenue
London NW5 2RZ

A catalogue record for this book is available
from the British Library

ISBN: 978-0-7112-3188-7

Printed in China

9 8 7 6 5 4 3 2 1

For Beth and Tom

HALF-TITLE PAGE: Although occasionally venturing inland the coast path mostly hugs the cliff tops, providing walkers with spectacular vantage points to enjoy the magnificent scenery.
TITLE PAGE: Viewed from the north shores of Woolacombe, the setting sun touches the horizon near Baggy Point.
OPPOSITE: Midway between the towns of Budleigh Salterton and Sidmouth the secluded little Ladram Bay is a geological feast for the eyes. Several pillars of red rock stacks stand just offshore from the beach, which is in turn backed by cliffs formed of the same red Otter Sandstone.

CONTENTS

FOREWORD

On its journey through four counties, the Coast Path runs along harsh windswept cliffs, through bustling seaside resorts and idyllic fishing villages, around dramatic promontories, through woodland and pastures and across sandy beaches. There really is a stretch of path to suit any ability and any mood. The light, the wildlife and of course the sea are constantly changing, so each walk along it brings fresh experiences.

Adam is a truly exceptional photographer, and his stunning pictures capture the wonderful contrasting scenery that makes the South West Coast Path National Trail a world class walk.

I hope that Adam's images of the South West Coast Path remind you of the exceptionally beautiful landscape of your walks. And if you haven't walked it all yet, inspire you to come back and visit the places you've missed.

It is also much appreciated that a proportion of the sale price of this book is being donated towards path improvement projects. If you would like any more information on the South West Coast Path please visit our website: www.southwestcoastpath.com

Mark Owen
National Trail Officer
South West Coast Path Team

Just west of Minehead the coast path ascends North Hill and meanders westwards, soon reaching Bossington Hill which offers spectacular views over Porlock Bay.

MAP

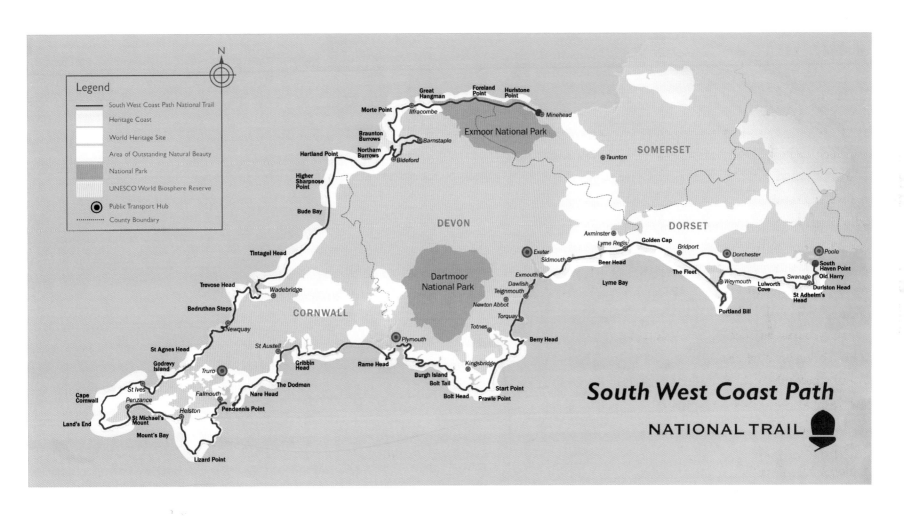

INTRODUCTION

Stretching for 630 miles all around the coast of south west England from Minehead to Poole, the South West Coast Path is Britain's longest way marked footpath. Its origins date back to the nineteenth century as a walking route, but in those days it was not used for recreational pursuits.

The long distance path running all along the windswept headlands and over remote coves began its existence with a very different purpose, to restrict smuggling. At this time it was estimated that half of all spirits consumed in England had been illegally brought into the country by smugglers. To counter this, Parliament decided that a network of connecting paths should be created to be patrolled by the newly formed Coastguard Service. In order for each Coastguard to effectively patrol for smuggling activity there needed to be unrestricted views of all coves, beaches and estuaries. These could only be gained if the paths were able to hug the cliff edges, regardless of any coastal properties.

Over time, the paths provided access ways for more than just the coastguards; their wives would use the paths to travel between villages and their children to travel to and from school. All this activity further defined the paths, making them a near permanent feature on the south west's cliff tops.

Ironically, it is fortunate indeed for us that smuggling resulted in such drastic action, as without it there would be little hope that today's coast path would run unhindered close to cliff tops and through private land.

The modern day coast path was completed in 1978, when the final section running between Somerset and North Devon was opened and designated a National Trail. It was in no small part due to the committed work of the South West Coast Path Association, a charity which campaigned to establish the path as we know it today.

Today the coast path is enjoyed by millions of visitors each year. Some come to challenge themselves walking the 630 mile route either in one endurance trek, or as a series of long distance walks. A great many more people enjoy shorter walks all along the path, marvelling at the unrivalled coastal scenery on offer.

And what scenery it is too! Over the full length of the trail, the coastline is utterly breathtaking and offers tremendous variety for all tastes. Even the cliffs themselves vary dramatically, from the rugged splendour of West Cornwall's granite and the dark slate of North Cornwall, to the soaring

The sculpture which marks the starting point of the coast path in Minehead.

cliffs of Exmoor and the various coloured cliffs along the Jurassic Coast of Devon and Dorset. Away from the cliffs, there are huge expanses of sandy beach such as Saunton Sands in Devon, and little known rocky coves such as Porth Nanven in Cornwall. For those looking for something less rugged, there are many waterways, like Fowey Estuary in Cornwall or Salcombe Estuary in Devon. And finally for those seeking picture postcard towns there are a plethora of beautiful fishing villages with ancient harbours to explore and relax in such as Clovelly in Devon or Mevagissey in Cornwall.

The south west benefits from some of the finest coastal scenery to be found anywhere in the world; thanks to the South West Coast Path this scenery can be enjoyed in an unbroken trail by visitors for many years to come.

At the northern end of Woolacombe, low tide merges the beach with Coombesgate. Where its better known neighbour is a vast length of unbroken golden sand, Coombesgate's beach is interspersed with dark rocks. On a retreating tide, the beach is left with beautiful reflective pools of water.

NORTH DEVON AND SOMERSET

The sun sets out to sea over Rockham Bay.
From the coast path Grey Seals can sometimes
be spotted swimming in the channels at the base
of these cliffs.

Weathered wooden groynes such as these are positioned along much of Exmoor's Bossington Beach and neighbouring Porlock Beach to prevent the actions of long shore drift. The pastel coloured smooth pebbles are pushed high up the beach by the tide, putting the wooden posts under tremendous pressure until eventually they break away.

On top of Castle Rock on Exmoor, a bird's eye vista provides a clear view into the rocky Wringcliff Bay below The Valley of Rocks. From here the coast path skirts around Duty Point and then returns to hug the towering cliff tops on the horizon at Highveer Point.

Overlooking Ilfracombe Harbour on one side and the rugged coast on the other, St Nicholas Chapel is perched atop Lantern Hill and is reputed to be the oldest working lighthouse in Britain. The building, which dates back to 1361, has been used as a lighthouse for around 650 years.

LEFT: (Top) The picture postcard Exmoor village of Lynmouth is captured at high tide early on a beautiful spring morning.
(Bottom left) In the late nineteenth century, Woody Bay was being promoted as the newest Victorian seaside resort in Devon. Roads and a railway station were built on the cliff tops, while a pier was built to accommodate coastal steamers. Unfortunately, bad weather destroyed the pier and the grand resort plans were abandoned soon after.
(Bottom right) Just past the western border of Exmoor National Park, Watermouth Cove is a delightfully secluded natural harbour. With protection on three sides and only a narrow entrance to the sea, the cove provides a sheltered mooring for many boats.

Morte Point has long been a notorious site for shipwrecks. Even the name, which translates as Death Point, conjures up a sense of foreboding and danger. As the coast path rounds the tip of Morte Point it turns abruptly south, heading for the sandy expanse of Woolacombe.

The coast path runs along the landward edge
of Braunton Burrows, the largest sand dune
system in England. The dunes are possibly
at their most picturesque nearer the sea,
where you can overlook the golden expanse
of Saunton Sands.

At low tide, a vast expanse of sandy beach is revealed at Westward Ho! Captured here at sunset, three figures stand at the water's edge, presumably preparing for some night time fishing.

Clovelly is a picture postcard fishing village set in idyllic surroundings. The village clings to the side of a heavily wooded cliff, its pretty cottages almost stacked on top of each other. A tiny and very steep cobbled lane meanders around the buildings before arriving at the water's edge beside a beautiful little walled harbour.

A tidal pool on the rocky shores
beneath Abbotsham Cliff.

One of the lesser known geological marvels to be found along the coast path, Blackchurch Rock is a double arched stack guarding the headland at Mouth Mill.

From Damehole Point a wonderful view can be achieved of the dramatic coastline of the Hartland Peninsula. Past the rocky Blegberry Beach the hotel on Hartland Quay is just about visible near the base of the cliffs.

Beneath a colourful sky these rocky ledges take on a steely cold appearance as twilight settles over Hartland Quay.

The broken and twisted bands of rock of the Hartland Peninsula provide some of the most dramatic scenery along the entire length of the coast path. The awe inspiring cliffs clearly show strata contorted at impossible angles, evidence of tectonic plate collision millions of years ago.

A colourful sunset over the rocky shores of secluded Speke's Mill Mouth and St Catherine's Tor.

NORTH CORNWALL

From the coast path at Porthcothan Bay
glorious views of the North Cornish coastline
extend all the way up to Trevose Head.

High tide washes clean the beach at Duckpool, a National Trust cove south of the Cornwall/Devon border. With the fierce waves of the North Atlantic crashing constantly upon these shores, the polished rocks are always on the move.

All over the wide expanse of Sandymouth Bay, eroded rock ledges stretch out towards the ocean. Pictured here just after sunset on a gloomy day, the ledges are covered by incoming waves, recorded as a misty blur by the camera.

South of Duckpool triangular rock ledges poke out of the sea at vertical angles, resembling the dorsal fins of monstrous sharks. These jagged natural structures help to convey the wildness of this stretch of Atlantic coast.

A dark and foreboding evening on the rugged shores of Crackington Haven, showing the imposing cliff face of Pencannow Point to the north (right) and the picturesque headland of Cambeak to the south (left).

From the coast path on the cliffs above Penally Point a spectacular vista opens up showing the natural inlet which leads to the small fishing village of Boscastle.

BELOW (left): Looking back to Boscastle from Penally Point, two stone breakwaters provide further shelter to the harbour from the dangers of the North Atlantic. These walls were built in 1584 by Sir Richard Grenville, the famous English sea captain and cousin of both Sir Walter Raleigh and Sir Francis Drake.

At Trebarwith Strand a narrow stream channels deeply through the slate beds and underneath this small natural bridge, before finally meeting the ocean. The igloo shaped island lying just offshore is named Gull Rock.

Being an old slate quarry the cliffs at Backways Cove have been shaped by human hands; rather unexpectedly this only seems to have added to their magnificence. A finger-like pillar of slate, left by the quarry workers, stands watch at the base of the cliffs, withstanding constant assault by the relentless Atlantic waves.

In late spring, many cliff tops along the coast path come vividly to life with colourful wildflowers. Pictured here on top of Rumps Point are carpets of beautiful pink Sea Thrift *(Armeria maritima)*.

BELOW(left): Situated on the Camel Estuary almost two miles inland from the Atlantic, the charming fishing port of Padstow is now a popular tourist destination. The coast path crosses the estuary from Rock to reach Padstow via the Black Tor ferry, before continuing north to Stepper Point.

Common bluebells *(Hyacinthoides non-scripta)*
flowering on the cliffs near Rumps Point.

Waves surge onto the deserted shores of Harlyn Bay
at high tide early on a spring morning.

A beautiful dawn sky emerges above
the lighthouse at Trevose Head. Below,
Atlantic waves crash into the humorously
named Stinking Cove.

Twilight descends over the rocky shores
of Porth Mear.

Whether viewed from the cliff tops or down on the sand, Bedruthan Steps is one of the most beautiful beaches in Cornwall. At high tide, the beach disappears completely and access is impossible as Atlantic waves surge around the many stacks and crash against the cliffs.

Gorgeous pink Sea Thrift wildflowers cling precariously close to the cliff edges near Porthcothan Bay.

A beautiful sunset develops above Trevaunance Cove,
close to the village of St Agnes.

By the time this engine house at Wheal Coates was opened in 1872, Cornwall was the premier tin mining field in the world. At its peak there were around two thousand tin mines throughout Cornwall, many reaching deep beneath the cliffs and stretching far out under the sea bed. However, by the late nineteenth century mining in Cornwall was in decline, and many Cornish miners began emigrating to South Africa, Australia and North America where their skills were highly sought after.

WEST CORNWALL

Located on the top of the granite headland, and just visible in this picture, is the famous Logan Rock. The rock is an 80 tonne boulder, which historically could be rocked easily by hand. In 1824 the rock was purposefully dislodged by a Royal Naval officer, Lieutenant Hugh Goldsmith and his crew. After a public outcry the Admiralty ordered Goldsmith to reposition the rock in its original location. This proved a monumental task which involved months of labour, but the rock was eventually moved back to its original position in front of thousands of spectators.

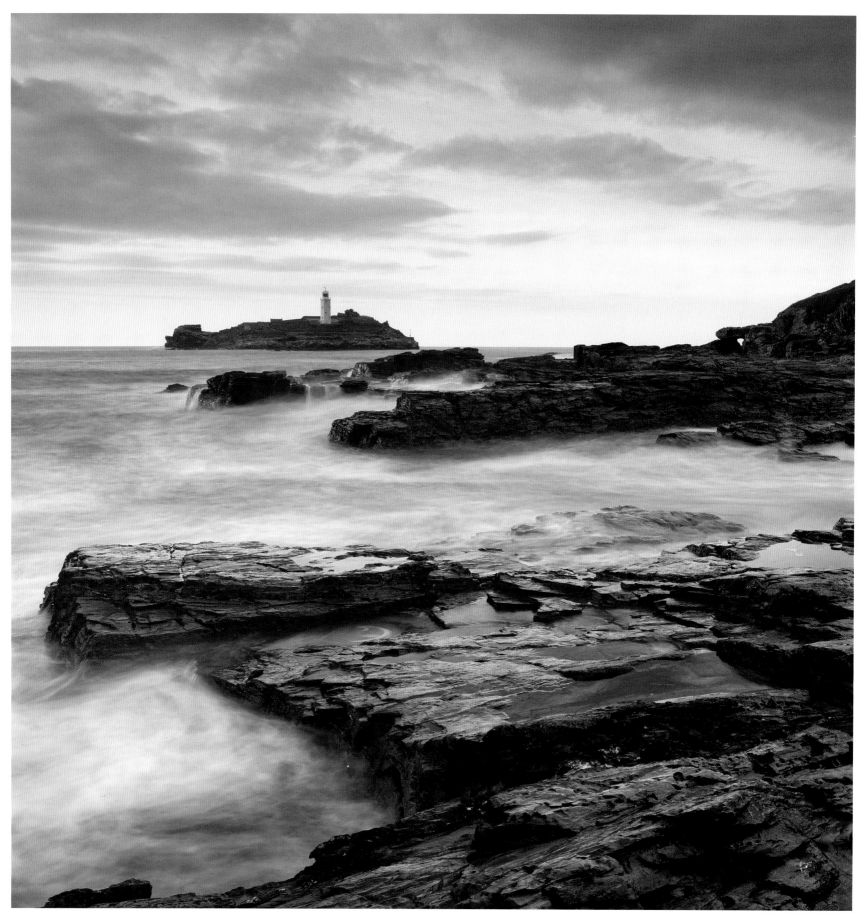

The Crown Mines engine houses, balanced precariously on the cliffs at Botallack, are further reminders of Cornwall's tin mining heritage. The mine itself stretches 400 metres out under the Atlantic, the deepest shaft being 500 metres below sea level.

BELOW: Originally a thriving fishing port, the picturesque St Ives is now primarily a holiday resort. It is a very popular location for artists, and is home to Tate St Ives gallery, a branch of the National Art museum The Tate.

OPPOSITE: Lying just off the rocky shores of Godrevy Point, Godrevy Lighthouse was built in 1859. The lighthouse was built to protect shipping from the dangerous reef The Stones, and was commissioned as a direct result of the sinking of the passenger ship SS Nile in 1854, with the loss of all souls on board.

Once thought to be the most south westerly point in mainland England, Cape Cornwall has long since conceded this accolade to nearby Land's End. Viewed here from the cliffs near the remains of the Iron Age Kenidjack Castle, it is easy to understand why such a mistake was made.

From the coast path on Mayon Cliff a dramatic vista opens up towards Land's End and the curiously named Dr Syntax's Head. The island at the base of the near cliffs is named the Irish Lady. Legend has it that the stack was named after the sole survivor of a shipwreck who clung to the rock awaiting rescue. Tragically before help arrived she was swept from the rock and drowned.

LEFT: (Top) At the outlet of the steep sided Cot Valley, lies the tiny little cove of Porth Nanven. The rounded granite boulders which are renowned on this beach have been sculpted by more ancient tides than those we witness today. These boulders have all fallen from the cliffs, where they would have previously been below sea level, over one hundred thousand years ago.
(Bottom) Stormy skies above Cape Cornwall and The Brisons Island, pictured from the sandy shores of Sennen Cove.

The most westerly point in mainland England, Land's End is also not surprisingly the most dramatic section of the whole coast path. Islands of eroded rock are scattered around the base of the soaring granite cliffs, and further afield. The most distant island being Longships, home to the lighthouse of the same name.

From the rocky cliff tops at Pordenack Point near Land's End the coast stretches south east in a series of spectacular granite headlands.

Late evening sunlight illuminates the cliffs and golden sands of beautiful Pednvounder Beach near Porth Curno.

Lying just offshore from Marazion,
St Michael's Mount is an iconic emblem of
Cornwall. With a rich historical background
as both a monastery and castle, this tidal
island can be walked to at low tide via
a stone causeway.

From the rocky shores of Church Cove the distant cliff top building reveals the location of the Poldhu Wireless Station, where Guglielmo Marconi transmitted the first transatlantic radio message in 1901. Until 1935, four towering masts dominated the headland immediately behind the former Poldhu Hotel, which is now possibly the finest located care home in Britain.

Located on the Lizard Peninsula, Mullion Cove is a picturesque harbour village in dramatic coastal surroundings. The coast path descends right through the village before climbing up Mullion Cliff to continue its journey towards Lizard Point.

At Lizard Point the coast path offers a sweeping view northwards back along the cliffs. Just visible near the distant headland are the white buildings and offshore islands of Kynance Cove.

A popular tourist destination since the Victorian era, Kynance Cove is considered one of the most beautiful beaches in the South West. Due to the unusual geology, at certain times the beach has two shores, with waves crashing behind and in front.

Another milestone of the South West Coast Path, Lizard Point marks the most southerly point on mainland Great Britain. Captured on a stormy spring evening this picture looks across the rocky waters of Polpeor Cove to Lizard Lighthouse and the former Lizard lifeboat station.

SOUTH CORNWALL

Late spring sees the many cliff top hawthorn trees near Dodman Point in beautiful white blossom. On top of the soaring 120 metre cliffs of The Dodman, the far reaching view stretches all the way to the Lizard Peninsula.

After rounding Lizard Point and neighbouring Housel Bay the coast path reaches Bass Point, where it abruptly turns north. This marks a very noticeable change in the sea, as the fierce Atlantic is replaced by the more sheltered waters of the English Channel.

RIGHT: A beautiful dawn sky emerges over the peaceful shores of Kennack Sands.

Vibrant pink Sea Thrift wildflowers cling to the rocky cliffs above Carrick Lûz in the springtime. Like many narrow promontories along the coast path, Carrick Lûz was once the location of an Iron Age hill fort.

Situated on the east side of the Lizard Peninsula, Coverack is a pretty coastal village surrounding a small working harbour. It is rumoured that some of the cottages still have secret passages and cellars from the days of smuggling.

This finely positioned cottage on Dolor Point enjoys a sweeping view over Perprean Cove towards the serpent like headland of Chynhalls Point.

From St Anthony Head on the Roseland Peninsula, a view stretches across Carrick Roads to the bustling port of Falmouth. Historically important as a port, Falmouth lays claim to having the third largest natural harbour in the world.

An early summer evening view looking west over Hemmick Beach towards Nare Head. This delightfully situated holiday cottage is owned by the National Trust and available to rent for the perfect coastal getaway.

RIGHT: After rounding The Dodman the coast path again turns in a northerly direction. Pictured here, the white sands of Vault Beach lead to Maenease Point. Just around the headland lies the little fishing village of Gorran Haven.

Named after two Irish saints, St Meva and St Issey, Mevagissey is one of Cornwall's most picturesque fishing villages. Fishing boats crowd the inner harbour, while rows of cottages, shops and restaurants overlook the waterfront.

On the far side of the Fowey Estuary lies the village of Polruan. With steep sided slopes Polruan provides shelter from the prevailing winds to the many yachts moored in Polruan Pool and nearby Pont Pill.

RIGHT: (Top) Glowing with golden light in the summer evening sunshine, the Church of St Fimbarrus enjoys beautiful surroundings in the heart of Fowey.

But things were not always so tranquil; the church, dating from 1460 is the third to stand on this location, the first being destroyed in the fourteenth century by pirates and the second by a French raid in 1456.

(Bottom): A stretch of lonely coast continues east from Polruan before finally the cliffs give way to the beautiful coastal village of Polperro. Scores of fishing boats crowd a little harbour surrounded by tightly packed fisherman's cottages, making Polperro a popular summer tourist destination.

Between Polperro and Looe, the quiet beach at Talland Bay provides a welcome change from the cliffs along this section of the coast path. In past centuries, this was a well known landing spot for smugglers.

At the far south eastern edge of Cornwall lies the vast sandy expanse of Whitsand Bay. Pictured here on a cold winter's evening, a colourful sunset begins to fade in the sky above Sharrow Point.

A late afternoon view of Whitsand Bay, looking eastwards towards the distinctive Rame Head from Freathy Cliff.

SOUTH DEVON

A beautiful sunset on a cold winter's day at Hope Cove. Waves surge over the sandy Shippen Beach, leaving beautiful patterns as the water retreats back into the sea.

The rocky shores of Wembury Bay look towards The Great Mewstone, a triangular shaped island jutting above the horizon. Now a bird sanctuary, the island has previously served as a prison. In 1744 a local man found guilty of a petty crime was sentenced to serve seven years on The Great Mewstone as an alternative to being transported to Australia.

Streetlights radiate warmth into this late evening view of Newton Ferrers, captured from the shores of neighbouring Noss Mayo. Located just off the Yealm estuary Newton Ferrers is an ancient village mentioned in the Domesday book. It was then simply known as Newton, but after being given to a Norman nobleman by the name of Ferrers, the village assumed its present day name.

BELOW: From the coast path high above Westcombe Beach, the rugged splendour of the South Hams stretch of coast becomes readily apparent.

On the beach itself, the geology is no less enthralling. Shark fin shaped rocks, encrusted with quartz veins, protrude from the dark sands all over Westcombe Beach.

Just around the cliffs from Bantham's sandy beach, the rocky ledges are eroded in smooth patterns from the passage of the tide over countless ages. Pictured here, the last glows of evening sunshine seem to turn the rocks to gold.

BELOW: The coast path descends into Soar Mill Cove via the curiously named Cathole Cliff. The cove is easily identifiable by the large teeth-like sea stacks, named Priest and Clerk, which guard the sea's entrance to the narrow beach.

After a misty start, rich sunlight finally breaks through to illuminate the flotilla of boats in Salcombe Estuary. Salcombe enjoys huge popularity as a destination for pleasure sailing, and as a result is a highly sought after location in the South Hams, with property prices among the highest in the UK.

RIGHT: A misty morning on the Kingsbridge Estuary, photographed from Scoble Point.

The turquoise sea laps gently against the deserted sandy shores of Elender Cove, protected from the prevailing winds by the mighty Gammon Head.

The southernmost tip of Devon, Prawle Point is also one of the most treacherous. Many ships have been wrecked here; as a result it is no surprise that the National Coastwatch Institution has a lookout station on the clifftops.

Arguably South Devon's most dramatic coastal scenery can be found on the Start Point promontory. The lighthouse was built in 1836 to alert nearby ships of the impending danger of the point and its offshore rocks.

Moored among the neat rows of boats in Brixham's picturesque harbour is one of England's most famous historical ships. In truth, the Golden Hind rotted away over three hundred years ago, but this full scale replica, permanently moored in Brixham, offers an authentic reproduction of Sir Francis Drake's famous ship.

RIGHT: Teignmouth's Grand Pier greets the ever warming sky on the first light of a new morning.

From the vantage point high up on the coast path above Littleham Cove, Straight Point's distinctive headland emerges through the morning mist. Nearby Orcombe Point signifies the start of the Jurassic Coast World Heritage Site, which now joins the coast path for almost all of the remaining journey to Poole Harbour.

The coast path travels over the striking red sandstone cliffs at High Peak, before descending into Sidmouth, where it follows the esplanade past the seafront houses.

Close to Devon's border with Dorset,
the pretty fishing village of Beer is crowded
around a small cove. Unusually for a fishing
village there is no harbour, instead the boats
are hauled up onto the steep pebbly beach each
evening after returning with their daily catch.

At Beer Head, the distinctive red sandstone suddenly gives way to equally unstable white chalk cliffs. Pictured here, foliage covers the Hooken landslide which occurred between 1789-90.

DORSET

The distinctive white cliffs of Old Harry Rocks
signifies the end of the Jurassic Coast World
Heritage Site which has followed the coast path
since Exmouth in Devon.

Stretching out into Lyme Bay, the beautiful curving harbour wall named The Cobb is the first of many instantly recognisable icons to be encountered on the Dorset stretch of the coast path.

At 626 feet Golden Cap is the highest point on the south coast of England. From the distinctive flat summit, far reaching views stretch for many miles along the coast and inland over beautiful rolling countryside.

As darkness descends over distant Lyme Regis, waves surge up the shingle beach at neighbouring Charmouth.

The distinctive yellow layered rocks of Burton Cliff are
best viewed away from the coast path on Burton Beach.
These cliffs are rich in fossils, which are occasionally
revealed after rockfalls.

As the coast path reaches Chesil Beach it veers suddenly to the left, away from the sea and up into the rolling Dorset countryside. It soon returns to sea level, but continues on the landward edge of the Fleet Lagoon, which looks across to Chesil Beach.

Mid way through circumnavigating Portland, the coast path reaches Portland Bill, a rugged outcrop at the southernmost tip of the island. The red and white banded lighthouse was built in 1906, and is visible many miles away, from the mainland.

Looking west from the coast path on the slopes of Swyre Head down over the Bat's Head outcrop. At the base of the headland a tiny natural arch, Bat's Hole is emerging as the cliff is eroded by the actions of the sea.

Another icon of the coast path, Durdle Door is a beautiful natural arch easily viewed from the coast path's cliff top vantage point. A popular bathing spot in summertime, it is at its most special in the winter when you may have the beach completely to yourself.

LEFT: Just on the other side of Durdle Door beach is the equally picturesque Man of War Bay.

A less familiar view of the shell shaped Lulworth Cove, captured from the eastern cliffs on a cold blue winter's dawn.

Huge waves crash high up on Worbarrow
Bay beach, casting long white trails as
the water rushes back into the sea.

After leaving Worbarrow Bay, the coast path climbs high along the soaring Gad Cliff, offering far reaching views over Brandy and Kimmeridge Bays, all the way towards St Aldhelm's Head.

The shores of Kimmeridge Bay on a dark and foreboding winter's evening. The headland folly, Clavell Tower has in recent years been dismantled and rebuilt several metres away from the cliff top, to protect it from coastal erosion.

After a heavy downpour the clouds suddenly break near St Aldhelm's Head, and rich evening light is bathed on the cliffs surrounding Chapman's Pool.

Looking south west from the coast path, back over the tiny cove at Winspit, its surrounding cliffs golden in the first sunlight of a new day. Unusually turbulent waves crash all over the rocky shore on this cold winter's morning.

A lonely sea stack named Parson's Barn stands proudly away from the headland just off Ballard Down.

With views stretching to Old Harry Rocks on the horizon, the sandy beach at Studland Bay provides the final stretch of the magnificent coast path. At its northern tip, where the beach meets Poole Harbour is South Haven Point, the official end point of the coast path, and the end point of our journey.

AUTHOR'S NOTES

Photographing the South West Coast Path presented me with a huge challenge. The scenery along the full length of the path could easily fill six books, so I knew I would have to tailor my approach to capturing photographs for the book. Early on I made a conscious decision to make this book an inspiring visual portrayal of the coast path, rather than a general guide book. To achieve this I decided on several things; firstly and most importantly I was going to allow myself to photograph from not only the coast path itself, but also from scenery around the path. This decision would allow me to use my creativity to fully capture the scenery that draws people to enjoy the coast path, and would also give the book a rich variety. So, as well as shooting from the clifftop vantage points, I also photographed from beaches, rocky coves and the occasional harbour.

My second decision was to showcase these locations in the best quality of light, which usually occurs around sunrise and sunset. At these times, before the day arrives or after most visitors have returned home, the coast becomes very special indeed, quiet and remote yet magical and memorable. It is for moments such as this that I return to the coast again and again.

The third major decision was not to force myself to photograph every location along the coast path. With such a wealth of spectacular scenery to fit into just over a hundred pages, it was never going to be possible to include every bay, cove, harbour and estuary. I could concentrate on the obvious and well known highlights, but I knew this would involve more towns than I was comfortable with in a book which, in essence celebrates our natural coastline. So instead I relied on map based research to help me to pin point stretches of the coast path which seemed to showcase the coastline at its finest, and often its wildest.

The sculpture marking the end of the coast path at South Haven Point by Poole Harbour.

The final factor in deciding on which locations went into the book was down to the quality of the photographs themselves. Whenever I struggled with a decision on which pictures to include I favoured quality of light over location. This meant that several better known areas didn't make the book, but ultimately being a picture book rather than a guide to the coast path, this seemed the most natural choice. This will no doubt mean that some peoples favourite locations have been omitted, but I hope that those people will also find new and exciting places to explore through viewing the other pictures.

The book has been sub divided into several chapters, which has effectively cut the coast path into sections. These sections are purely to make the book more manageable to navigate, and do not have any other significance.

The Isle of Portland has for a long time been used for quarrying. Many of the finest buildings in London, including St Paul's Cathedral and parts of Buckingham Palace are built using stone from the island.

INDEX